LET'S LOOK AT SHARKS

Malcolm Penny

Language Consultant
Diana Bentley
University of Reading

Artist
Wendy Meadway

The Bookwright Press
New York · 1990

Let's Look At

First published in the United States in 1990 by
The Bookwright Press
387 Park Avenue South
New York NY 10016

First published in 1989 by
Wayland (Publishers) Limited
61 Western Road, Hove, East Sussex, BN3 1JD, England

© Copyright 1989 Wayland (Publishers) Limited

Library of Congress Cataloging-in-Publication Data
Penny, Malcolm
   Let's look at sharks/by Malcolm Penny: [artist, Wendy Meadway].
      p. cm. – (Let's look at)
   Bibliography: p.
   Includes index.
   Summary: An introduction to sharks, the different types,
and their habits and behavior.
   ISBN 0–531–18308–4
   1. Sharks – Juvenile literature. [1. Sharks.] I. Meadway,
Wendy, ill. II. Title. III. Series: Let's look at (New York, N.Y.)
QL638.9.P43 1990
597′.31 – dc 19   89–31200
                                                        CIP
                                                        AC

Printed by Casterman S.A., Belgium

Words printed in
bold are explained
in the glossary.

Contents

Help! Sharks!

Most people are afraid of sharks, because they think that sharks will **attack** people who go swimming. In some parts of the world big sharks are dangerous, but there are many

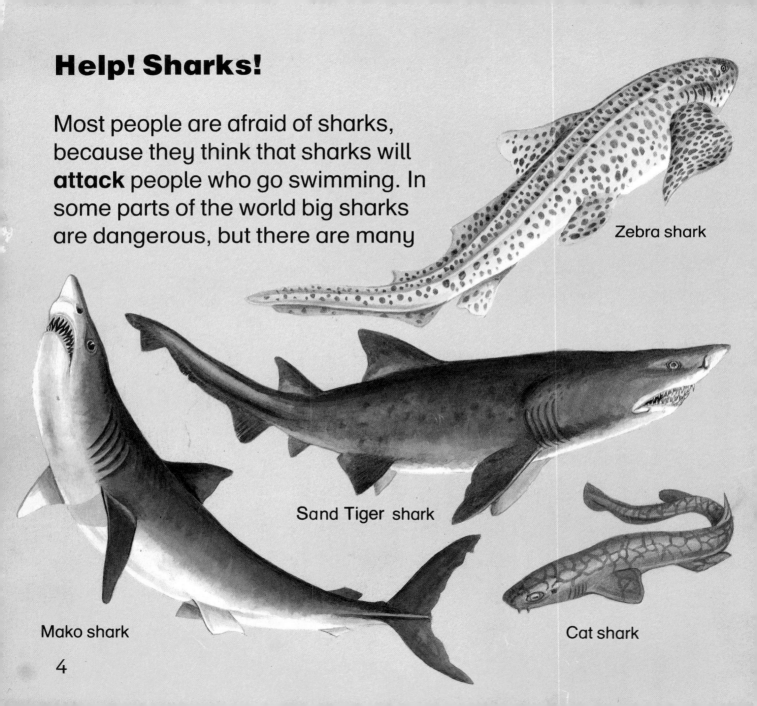

Zebra shark

Sand Tiger shark

Mako shark

Cat shark

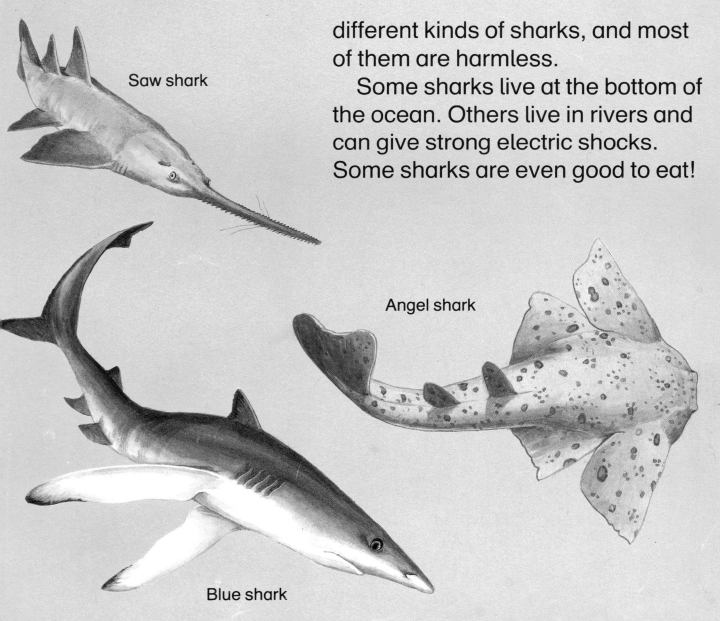

Saw shark

different kinds of sharks, and most of them are harmless.

Some sharks live at the bottom of the ocean. Others live in rivers and can give strong electric shocks. Some sharks are even good to eat!

Angel shark

Blue shark

What is a shark?

Sharks are fish, but sharks are different from fish like cod or herring because they have soft bones.

Tiger shark

Nostril

Eye

Gill openings

Fin

Tail

Fin

Mouth

Fins

Fins

Like other fish, they use **gills** to breathe under water. A shark's skin is very tough and covered with tiny **spines**. All sharks are hunters, but not all of them are fierce. Some of them only hunt snails or shrimps.

Sharks' teeth grow in rows, so that as the front ones are worn out or broken off, new ones come forward to replace them.

Front of mouth

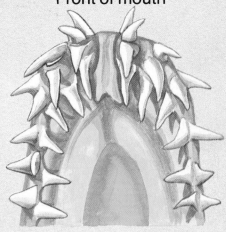

Looking down on rows of teeth waiting to come forward

How a shark breathes

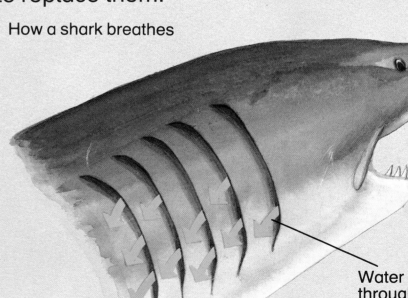

Water is taken in through the mouth

Water is filtered out through gill openings

The great white shark

Great white sharks are really gray
or brown on top, but they are white
underneath. They are found in warm
seas all around the world. They can
grow up to six meters (20 ft) long.

They have sharp, triangular teeth, and they are very fierce. Their usual food is fish, seals and dolphins, but they sometimes attack and eat people. They follow ships to eat any garbage thrown overboard.

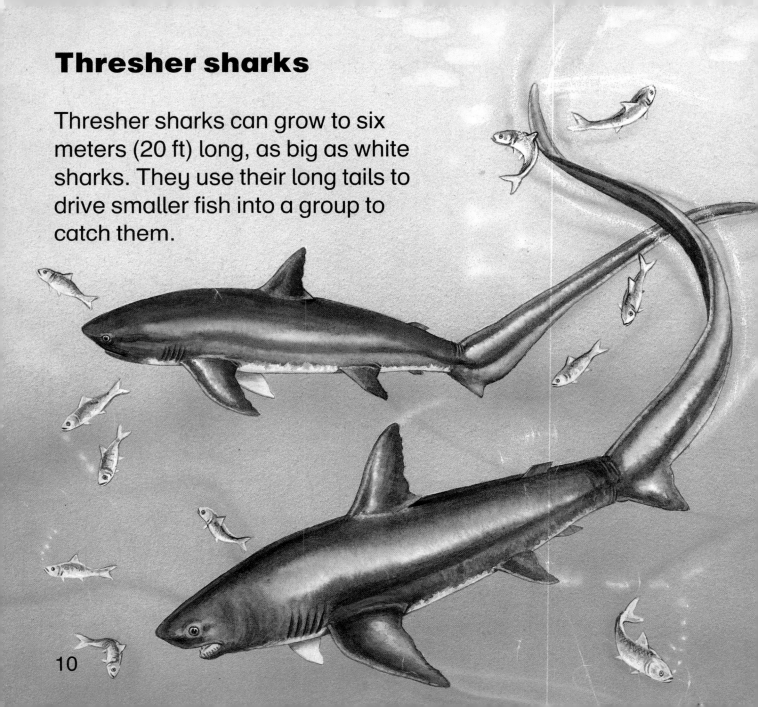

Thresher sharks

Thresher sharks can grow to six meters (20 ft) long, as big as white sharks. They use their long tails to drive smaller fish into a group to catch them.

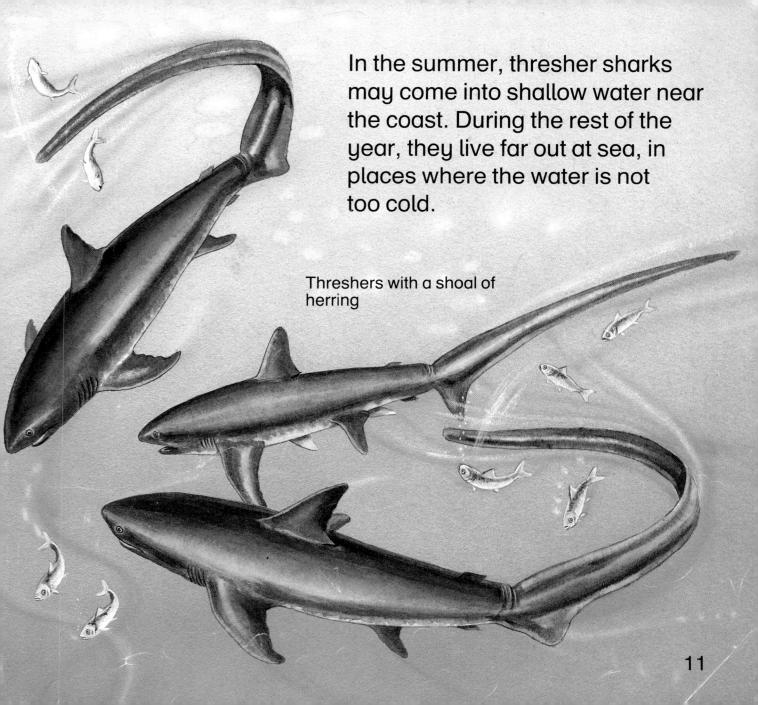

In the summer, thresher sharks may come into shallow water near the coast. During the rest of the year, they live far out at sea, in places where the water is not too cold.

Threshers with a shoal of herring

Hammerhead and whale sharks

A hammerhead shark has its eyes at the ends of thick **stalks**, which makes its head look like a hammer. Hammerheads live in warm parts of the world. They often come close to the beach. They usually eat fish or squid.

Hammerhead shark

Whale shark

12

Whale sharks live far out in deep, warm seas. They are the biggest of all fish, and can grow to over 15 meters (50 ft) long. They move slowly, and they are harmless. They feed by straining small fish and shrimps out of the water.

The divers look very small next to the huge whale shark

Dogfish

Dogfish are small sharks. They are only about 80 centimeters (31 in) long. They live in cool seas. They feed on the bottom, mostly on worms and shellfish.

The empty shells of their eggs are called "mermaid's purses" when they are washed up on beaches. Like many sharks, dogfish are good to eat. They are called "rock salmon" in some fish stores.

Dogfish

15

Rays

Rays are part of the shark family, although they are very different in shape. They are triangular, and they flap their wings to fly like birds under the water.

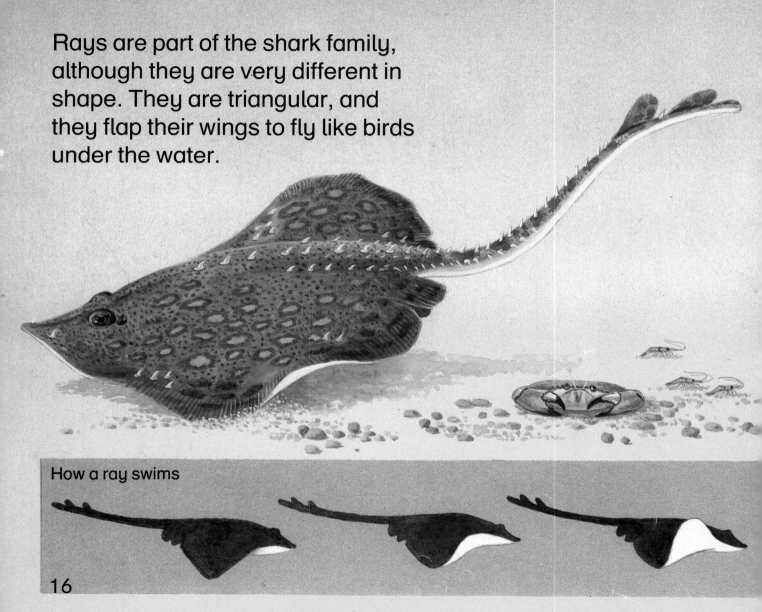

How a ray swims

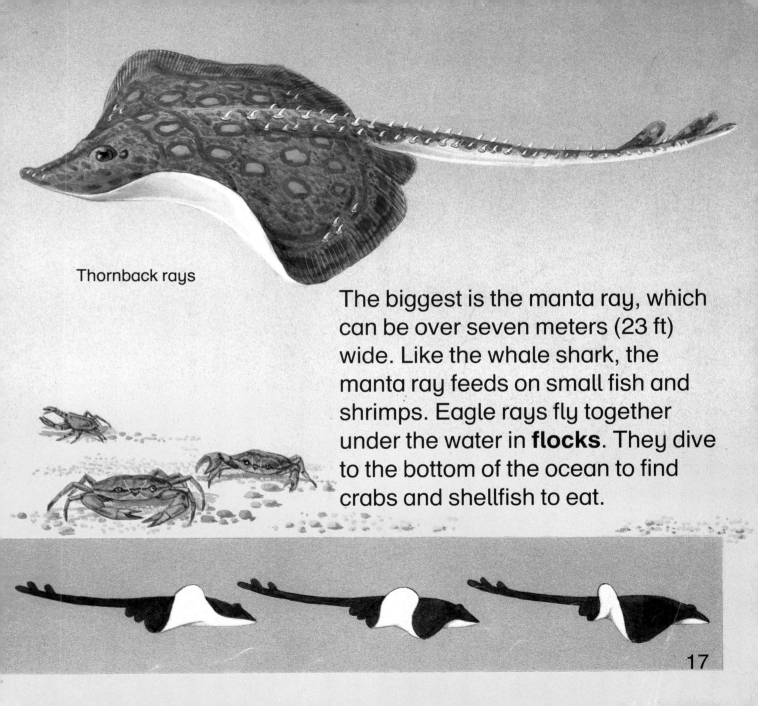

Thornback rays

The biggest is the manta ray, which can be over seven meters (23 ft) wide. Like the whale shark, the manta ray feeds on small fish and shrimps. Eagle rays fly together under the water in **flocks**. They dive to the bottom of the ocean to find crabs and shellfish to eat.

17

Two strange sharks

The electric ray is a very strange member of the shark family. It lives in rivers or very deep in the ocean. It cannot see to hunt in the muddy water so it finds its **prey** by feeling with its fins. Then it kills its food with a strong electric shock.

A fish swims over a partly-hidden electric ray

The wobbegong looks like a rug. It is sometimes called a carpet shark. It lives among **coral**, in warm shallow water. It eats shellfish such as periwinkles and clams.

Wobbegong shark

19

How sharks swim

Rays "fly" through the water like birds, but the hunting sharks move differently. Their tails sweep from side to side to drive them along, and their front fins work like stiff wings to keep them up.

Gray sharks in an aquarium

Sharks cannot float. If they stop swimming, they sink. One shark in an **aquarium** in Australia swam around its tank without stopping for four years. In that time, it traveled 160,000 kilometers (99,000 mi).

How sharks hunt

The swift hunting sharks find their prey by feeling movements in the water. They can tell if a fish or a seal is wounded or trying to escape. Sharks attack these animals.

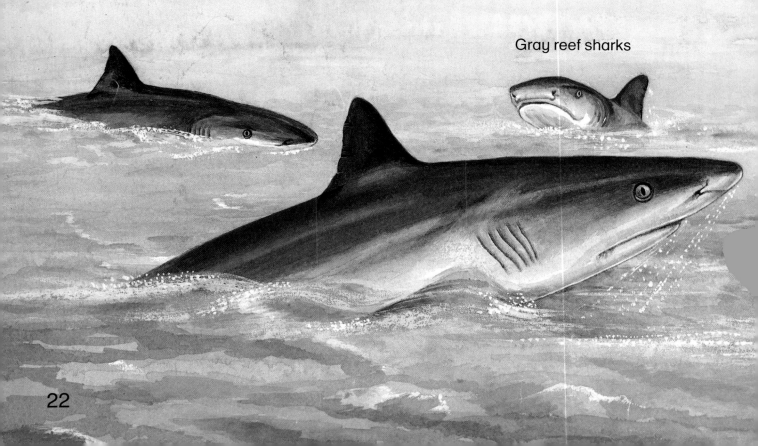

Gray reef sharks

Sharks can also smell their prey in the water, from a long way away. When a shark attacks, it raises its head to open its mouth very wide. Then it bites and shakes its prey to cut pieces off it.

What sharks eat

All sharks eat other animals. The big hunting sharks eat seals and sea lions, dolphins and even small whales. The smaller ones eat fish or squid.

Crocodile shark feeding

Great white shark chasing a dolphin

24

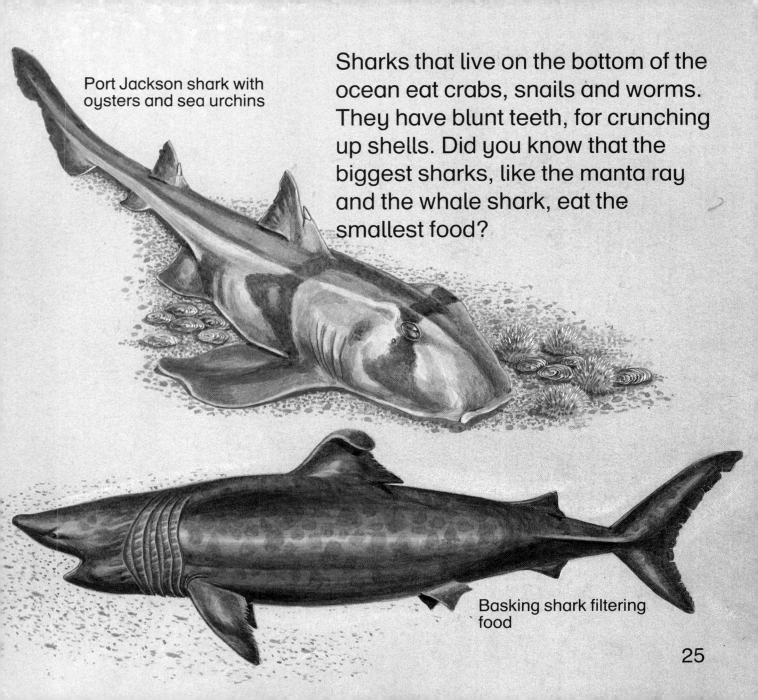

Port Jackson shark with oysters and sea urchins

Sharks that live on the bottom of the ocean eat crabs, snails and worms. They have blunt teeth, for crunching up shells. Did you know that the biggest sharks, like the manta ray and the whale shark, eat the smallest food?

Basking shark filtering food

25

Sharks and their babies

Some sharks have babies, which grow inside their mother until they are ready to be born.

A lemon shark gives birth. The diver holds one of the newly born pups

Other sharks lay eggs. The eggs have long curly strings to fix them to rocks until they hatch. The young sharks swim away in search of food. Some mother sharks do not lay their eggs, but let them hatch inside their bodies.

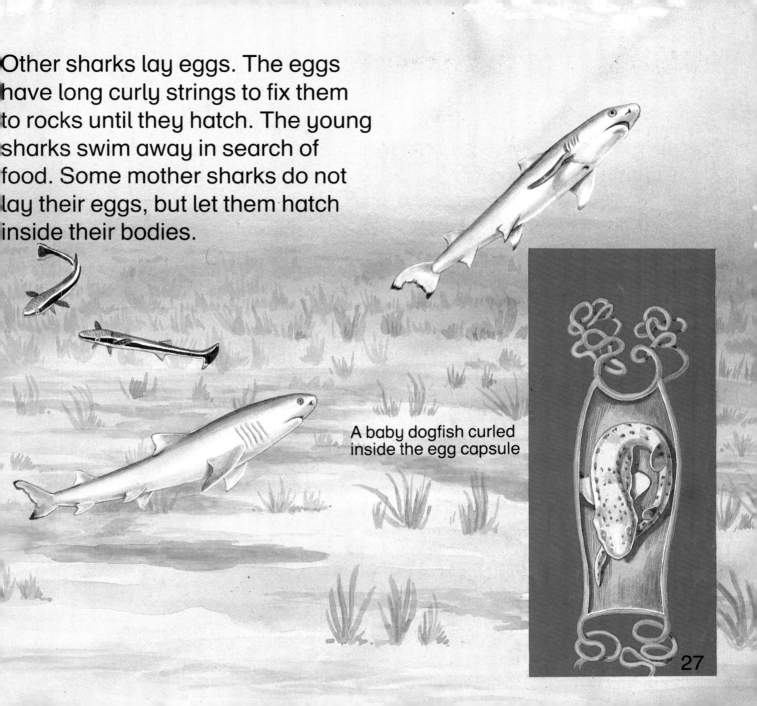

A baby dogfish curled inside the egg capsule

Sharks and people

Great white sharks are not the only ones that are dangerous to people. Hammerheads, blue sharks and sand sharks may all attack if they have the chance.

In warm countries, there is often a net in the ocean to keep sharks away from beaches where people swim. Many small sharks, such as dogfish and Mako, are good to eat. Some Chinese people use shark fins to make a special soup.

Sharks are being studied by scientists, so that we can learn more about them.

Nets keep sharks away from swimmers on this Australian beach

Glossary

Aquarium   A pool in which animals are kept so that we can go to look at them.

Attack   To hurt or harm something.

Coral   A growth which looks like a plant and lives on rocks and the floor of warm seas.

Flock   A large group of animals of one kind.

Gills   The parts of a fish through which it breathes.

Prey   An animal hunted or captured by another animal for food.

Spines   Hard-pointed parts of the shark's skin.

Stalks   Stem-like parts the head of the hammerhead shark.

Books to read

Sharks, by Kate Petty (Franklin Watts, 1985).
Sharks, by Alwyne Wheeler (Gloucester Press, 1987).
The World of Sharks by Andrew Langley (Bookwright Press, 1988).

Index